D1047099

Man Meets Woman

A book by Yang Liu

Humans, so one Chinese legend tells us, were created by a female divinity. At first she made them sexless and completely identical. Only when they consequently failed to produce offspring did the goddess later furnish them with gender. According to the Bible, humans were created by a male God—first man, then woman. The world of science in turn offers us an entirely different version of the origins of humankind.

I myself have experienced, directly and indirectly, many communication problems between the two sexes, both in my private life and in my professional career. As a working wife and mother, I am compelled to realize time and time again how many minor and major differences exist between men and women, despite today's ongoing debate on the subject and the constant redefinition of male and female roles. Many of these differences arise out of traditional gender models and are dictated by social and professional structures.

With this little book I would like to present a visual documentary of my personal views on the subject of communication between men and women. I thereby hope to be able to encourage all of us to approach this subject with a little more humor and, in our daily interactions, to look at and think about things from the viewpoint of the opposite sex.

Yang Liu

man to man

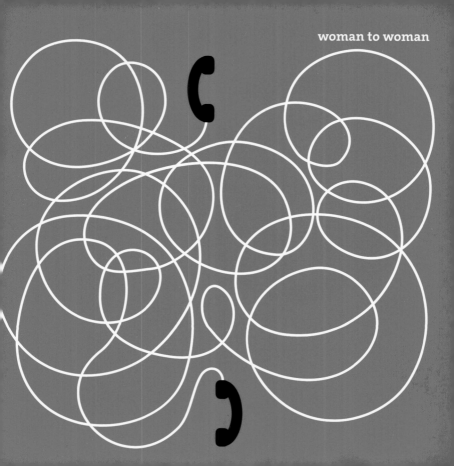

woman to woman

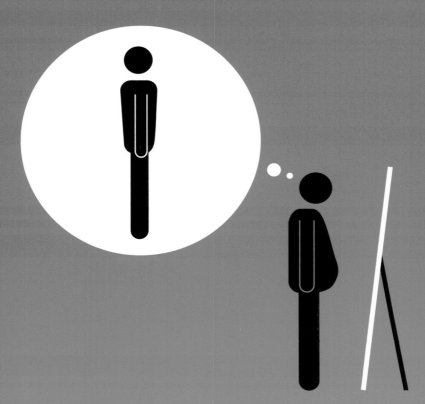

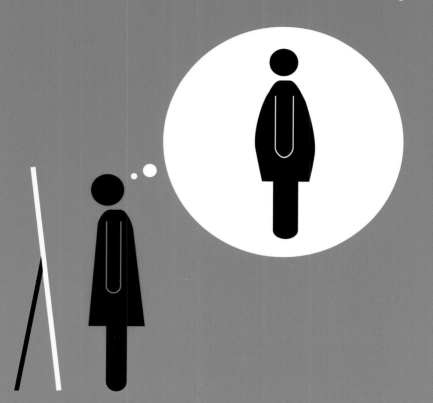

self-image

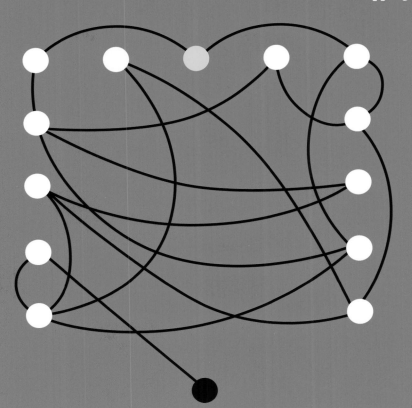

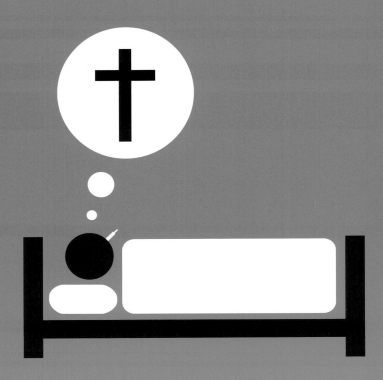

man flu

private talk

business talk

business talk

need

buy

need

buy

need

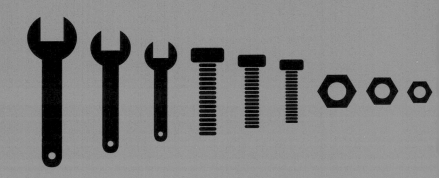

buy

need

buy

single focus

multitasking

shopping as a single

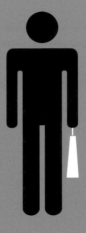

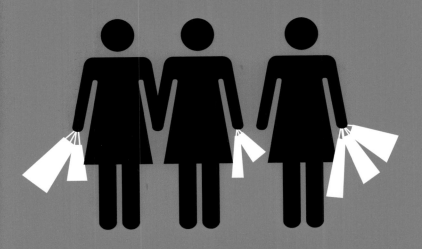

shopping as a single

shopping as a couple

shopping as a couple

mysterious objects

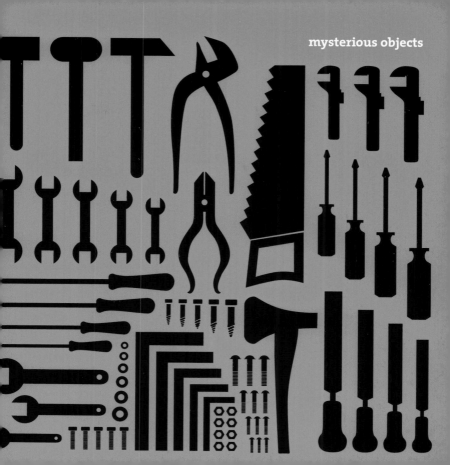

best weapon

when she's silent

finding the way

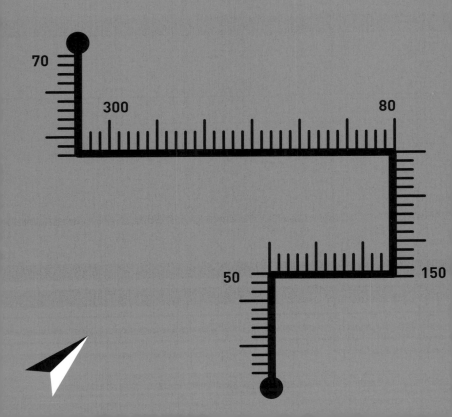

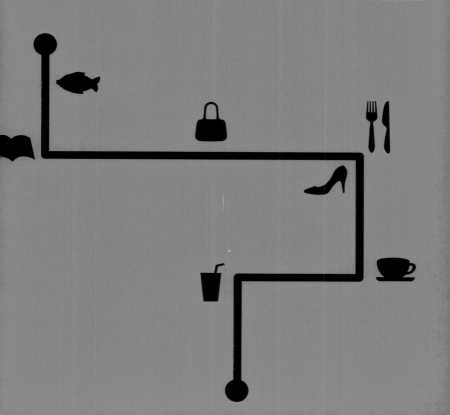

good to go

good to go

bathroom break

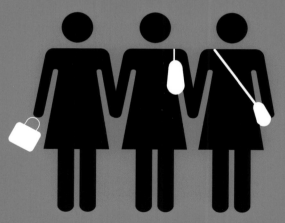

luggage

Melodrama

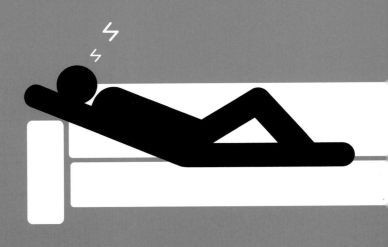

action movie

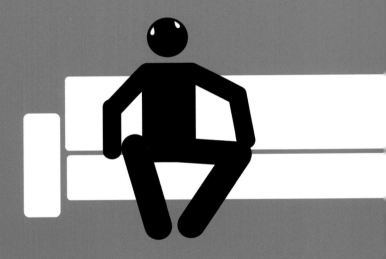

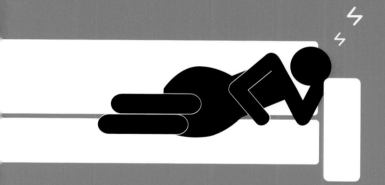

getting ready to go out

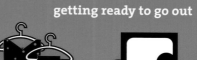

perfect evening

perfect evening

projected dream woman

15   **20**   **30**

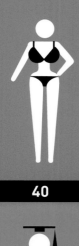

40   50   60

projected dream man

favorite drink

21   25   30

35　　　　　40　　　　　50

favorite drink

ideal age for marriage

25   30   40

18   25   30

18   25   30

50 60 18

40 50 60

40 50 60

ideal age for marriage

date

sexual experience

love

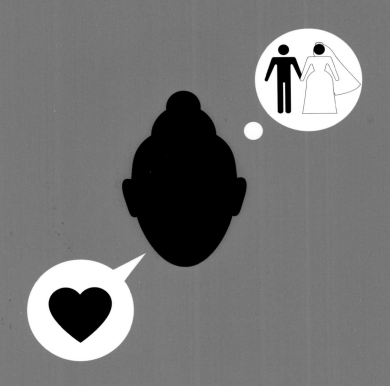

marriage

speaking about children

baby

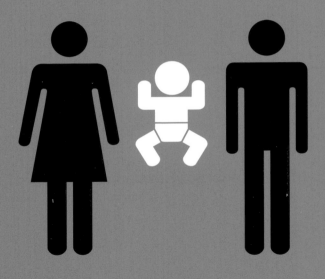

baby arrives

before

after

baby arrives

before

after

social presence – man loves man

he wants him

competition

successful man's prospects

successful woman's prospects

dream woman

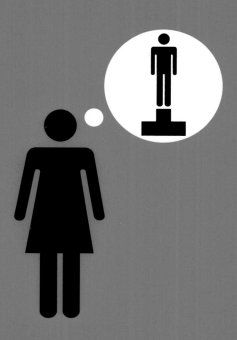

dream woman of a successful man

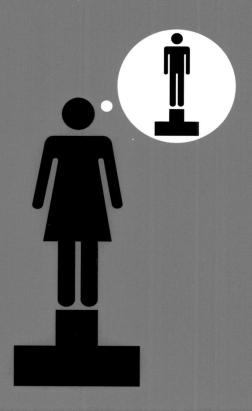

what others think

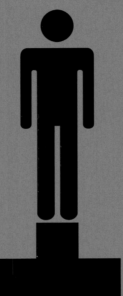

salary expectations

preferred boss

preferred boss

family man

workaholic

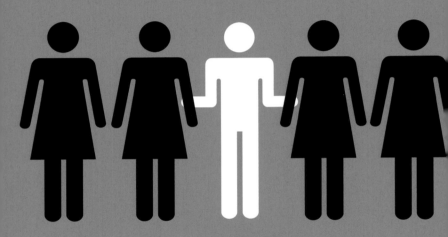

prince charming

whore

modern man

housewife

violent

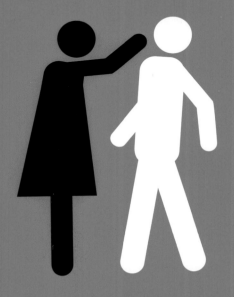

feisty

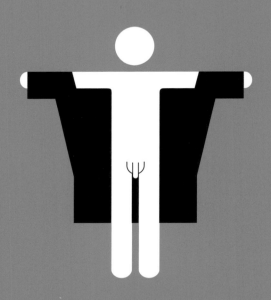

creepy

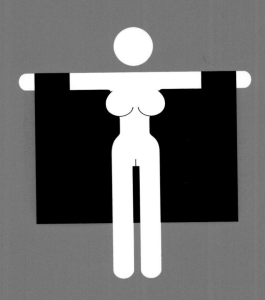

sexy

pervert

bold

macho

strong woman

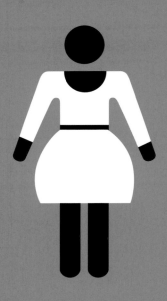

weird man

normal woman

he thinks that she thinks...

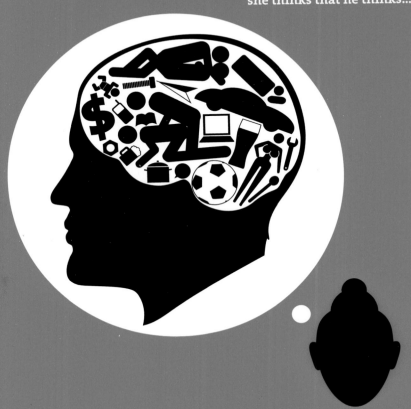

she thinks that he thinks...

In 2008 I had the idea of making a book about the differences between the sexes. I wanted to take stock of my thoughts and observations on the subject of Man/Woman as a way of documenting another stage of my life. It took six years for the book to assume its present shape.

We are living in an age of constant social change, in which the subject of the sexes, in particular, is rapidly evolving in people's consciousness. Each new generation re-assesses and questions the role models current-ly in place. All over the world, people are striving to break down exist-ing structures and are taking a stand for greater tolerance and equality, including in areas such as sexual orientation, culture, and religion.

It is interesting to see how Man/Woman clichés have indeed changed in our daily lives and to what extent the attributes that were assigned to the sexes in the past, often centuries ago, are still relevant in today's society. And to consider which desirable role models are already rooted in our thinking but are still in the process of transformation.

I hope to present a worthy successor to *East Meets West* and to continue exchanging thoughts and ideas with my readers on this topic and many others.

ng Liu was born in 1976 in Beijing. After studying at the Berlin
University of the Arts, she worked as a designer in Singapore, London,
rlin and New York. In 2004 she founded her own design studio,
hich she continues to run today. In addition to holding workshops
d lectures at international conferences, she has taught at numerous
universities in Germany and abroad. In 2010 she was appointed a
ofessor at the BTK University of Applied Sciences in Berlin. Her
orks have won numerous prizes in international competitions and
n be found in museums and collections all over the world.

ng Liu lives and works in Berlin.

Acknowledgments

Onno Zhang
Gong Zhang
Jürgen Siebert
Axel Haase
Benedikt Taschen
Marlene Taschen
Florian Kobler
Angela Kesselring
Susanne Reiher
Hui Bao Chang
Andreas Zumschlinge
Jan Bernd Nordemann
Katharina Wickert
Wolfram Wickert
Nils Schröder
Frank Sieren
Lucas Trabert
Gerry Kunz
Bin Qiu

Thank you all for your support!

Special thanks go to my *East Meets West*
readers, who have encouraged and
supported me with their many letters
and emails over the years.

To stay informed about upcoming
TASCHEN titles, please subscribe
to our free TASCHEN Magazine at
www.taschen.com/magazine,
find our Magazine app for iPad
on iTunes, follow us on Twitter
and Facebook, or e-mail us at
contact@taschen.com.

Man Meets Woman
A book by **Yang Liu**

Idea/Design © Yang Liu

© All artwork
and text copyright
Yang Liu Design
Torstraße 185 · 10115 Berlin
www.yangliudesign.com

Project Management:
Florian Kobler, Berlin
Production:
Frauke Kaiser, Cologne
English translation:
Karen Williams,
Rennes-le-Château

© 2014 TASCHEN GmbH
Hohenzollernring 53
D–50672 Cologne
www.taschen.com

ISBN 978-3-8365-5398-8

Printed in Italy